AF485194

Becoming Fearless

65 Strategies to Journey from Self-Doubt to Self-Mastery

Becoming Fearless

65 Strategies to Journey from
Self-Doubt to Self-Mastery

DR. BENJAMIN RITTER

Copyright © 2024-2026 by Benjamin Ritter, EdD, MBA, MPH

Becoming Fearless: 65 Strategies to Journey from Self-Doubt to Self-Mastery

Published by Live for Yourself Consulting LLC

All rights reserved. No part of this may be reproduced, distributed, or transmitted in any form or by any electronic or mechanical means, without permission in writing from the copyright owner except in the case of brief quotations embodied in critical reviews and certain non-commercial uses permitted by copyright law.

ISBN 979-8-9910603-0-1 paperback
ISBN 979-8-9910603-1-8 eBook

Acknowledgments

To my fear: without you, this book would never have existed.

To my sister and master wordsmith, Rachel Ritter, an infinite amount of thanks are bestowed in your direction.

To everyone in my life, thank you for standing by my side, through facing my fears, becoming fearless, and everything that life is in between.

Table of Fearlessness

Introduction

**Everything you want can be yours
when you become fearless.**

Imagine…

Having no limits.

Never doubting yourself.

Always being able to make the most of situations.

What if you could go to bed every night without worrying about tomorrow? If you could live without fear, every path would be open to you.

This book will show you how you can get there.

Fear is holding you back

If you picked up this book, there is some part of your life that is limited due to fear. Perhaps it's a career shift you dream of, a relationship that needs to end, or a goal that feels just out of reach. But whenever you actually think about doing something, your body and mind scream "Danger!" Your heartbeat races, your chest tightens, and your breath quickens. You label these feelings as fear, and let them hold you back.

Fear is not a fact

Fear is a *feeling* that has been defined by your *thoughts* – based on what you *believe* it represents.

We often misrepresent the feeling of fear as a sign of danger, which leads us to find reasons for being afraid. This traps us in a fear cycle: discomfort arises, we label it as fear, and then we convince ourselves that we are in danger because of it. Which reinforces and starts the loop again. We then try to avoid the discomfort, the changes, or goals, to feel safe. But this just keeps us stuck exactly where we started.

For example: Imagine wanting to start a business because you are feeling unfulfilled at work. You might feel nervous about leaving your job – *discomfort*. Then label the nervousness as a concern of failure – *fear*, which may convince you that starting a business is too risky – *danger*.

To avoid this fear, you decide not to pursue your business idea, which leaves you stuck and unfulfilled in your current job. The cycle occurs because we are trying to avoid something that isn't real.

Fear is just information, labeled in a way that doesn't serve us – a threat. The greatest lie we tell ourselves is that avoiding fear keeps us safe when it actually limits our potential.

You have to act

If you live your life believing your fear, listening when it tells you "don't," it will be impossible to change. The only way to overcome fear is to challenge it. To feel fear, and get curious. To act and see what happens, and then keep going.

Fearlessness comes from choosing to explore the unknown, rather than staying stuck in the comfort of what you know. As you take action, the perceived risks will diminish, and you will feel less fearful. You'll discover and start to believe that the risks aren't real or at least nothing to be really worried about.

Important terms

The insights and actions throughout this book are focused on challenging the feelings, thoughts, and beliefs that hold you back and create many of your fears. For our purposes, these terms are defined as follows:

Feelings: Instinctive emotional reactions to your circumstances/specific situation, influenced by what you think and believe about that emotion.

Thoughts: Ideas and/or opinions in your mind, developed to understand or assess something, influenced by what you feel and believe about those things.

Beliefs: What you accept as truth, influenced by what you think and feel about that idea over time.

Fear: a feeling defined by your thoughts, supported by a belief that something is dangerous or a threat.

How to use this book

The book is split into two different sections: Personal and Professional.

The *Personal* section offers tips to conquer fears affecting your Mindset, Success, Relationships, and Meaning.

The *Professional* section offers tips to conquer fears that impact your Job satisfaction, Leadership Presence, and Career Growth.

The tips in this book will resonate differently with every reader based on personal experiences and needs. With that in mind, the book is designed to be flexible – you can read and apply its insights in any order that resonates with you.

These tips provide straightforward – not easy – strategies for conquering your fears. When a particular tip resonates with you, dedicate time to practice it over the next few days, or until you notice a positive change in how you manage the specific fear.

As an additional resource to taking action and working on each tip, download the **Becoming** app, the daily practice behind this philosophy. liveforyourselfconsulting.com/becomingfearless.

Focus on improving one area at a time and try not to worry about the other tips until you feel satisfied. After noticing improvement, move on to another tip that speaks to you. The journey will take time, but this book equips you with the necessary tools.

You can become fearless

If you've picked up this book, you have already decided that fear is getting in your way and you are ready for a change. When you commit to taking action despite your fear, everything you want will be within your reach. It's time to become fearless.

Personal

You are fearless when you…

Conquer your fears

Are you making excuses instead of taking action?

We all experience fear and often blame it for not taking action. Our fear causes self-doubt and tends to be labeled as a risk or something to be avoided. However, it doesn't have to be viewed this way.

The feelings you think represent fear, are just pieces of information about your experiences. You create fear in response to a stimulus. It is a data point and not a fact. You get to decide what that information means.

Find reasons to take action:

To face your fear, you need to use the data that fear provides in a way that serves you, instead of against you. Fear can just as easily mean GO, instead of STOP or RUN.

The next time you feel fear, decide to reexamine the situation. Write your fear down so you can get it out of your head. Question or challenge your beliefs and find reasons for the actions you want to take. Just as you convince yourself to be afraid, prove to yourself that you have nothing to be afraid of. If you let fear limit your actions, you are allowing it to be more important than what you are trying to accomplish.

Just as you convince yourself to be afraid, prove to yourself that you have nothing to be afraid of.

You are fearless when you…

Feel your feelings

Do you try to avoid your emotions?

Uncomfortable emotions can seem easier to ignore than to feel. However, distancing ourselves from our emotions hinders our understanding of our experiences and ourselves, and tends to perpetuate or strengthen the feelings we try to avoid.

Examine what you feel:

When you feel uncomfortable emotions, instead of avoiding them, try to feel them. Pay attention to all the different reactions you are experiencing that are tied to the emotions. Ask yourself: "What is happening in my body?"

Allow yourself to become more aware of how these feelings are affecting you. Try to explore the feeling independent of anything else, such as negative labels or judgments.

If you don't label something as bad right away, then you are less likely to avoid it, and most importantly, learn something new about yourself.

**When you feel uncomfortable emotions,
instead of avoiding them,
try to feel them.**

You are fearless when you…

Choose how you feel

Do you often wish you could change how you feel?

When our emotions are negative, it's hard not to dwell on them. Despite the desire to feel differently, we find ourselves reacting to these emotions, letting them dictate our actions.

In these moments, you are doing one specific thing – you are trusting and reinforcing that what you feel is true. If you want to change how you feel, you need to stop accepting that your feelings define you.

Act how you want to feel:

Your emotions do not need to dictate your actions. You can choose to act despite your emotions, and those actions can transform how you feel.

Consider this: When you are feeling down, instead of focusing on the negative feeling and finding reasons for why you should feel that way, take action to create fun and more positive experiences.

When you want to change how you feel, focus instead on changing your actions, and your feelings will follow suit.

When you want to change how you feel,
focus instead on changing
your actions.

You are fearless when you…

Create a life that helps you feel good

Are you constantly in a bad mood?

Life should not be an endless loop of negativity. It's easy to miss out on the obvious things that create negativity in our lives, especially if they are part of our routines.

If you are often struggling with negative emotions, even fear, then how you are living – who and what you are surrounding yourself with – needs to change.

Cut out the negative:

Make a list of the times you feel unhappy or struggle throughout your day. Note the places, people involved, time of day, and the details of the situation.

Identify any potential reasons and themes that may be contributing to your negative feelings. Look for similarities between negative experiences such as certain people or topics, and then take steps to cut them out of your life or change your engagements with them.

As you distance yourself from negativity, you will curate an environment that fulfills you, instead of drains you.

Look for similarities between negative experiences such as certain people or topics, and then take steps to cut out or change them.

You are fearless when you…

Think about your thoughts

Do you struggle with intrusive thoughts?

Too often, we move through our days, rushing from task to task, too busy to reflect. We survive on autopilot through a combination of routine and reaction. We react to our thoughts – especially our fears – trusting them to be true, which then allows them to derail our day.

Change what you tell yourself:

When an intrusive thought interrupts your day, instead of accepting or pushing it away, take a moment to review the thought – word for word – before reacting. Then, challenge and rewrite the thought to serve you better. Literally, write the thought down, and then say the new thought out loud.

Choose to interpret your situations in a different way. For example, if you think you are nervous in a situation, decide to tell yourself that you are excited. The feelings may be the same, but the way you define and think about the situation is different.

When you actively redefine and reinforce your thoughts, you can rise above them and gain more control over yourself.

When an intrusive thought interrupts your day, instead of accepting or pushing it away, take a moment to review the thought – word for word – before reacting.

You are fearless when you…

Don't believe your beliefs

Is what you believe holding you back?

If you are struggling to make changes in your life, you are likely stuck on an old belief pattern. Belief patterns are programs we follow subconsciously. They are stories we tell ourselves over time, influenced by repeated thoughts. Eventually, they become ingrained as truths, underlying our decisions and actions. But since they are just stories we've decided to believe, we can also decide not to let them dictate our actions.

Reject beliefs that don't serve you:

Identify something you want to achieve but haven't made progress on. Explore your reason or excuse for not taking action and define the underlying belief that is holding you back. Create a new supportive belief that might motivate you to take action. For example, if going to the gym scares you because you believe that everyone will judge you, try a temporary belief for a week: everyone's too focused on their own workout to notice you. Repeat this belief as often as possible. Write it down, speak it out loud, and share it with others. When you frame the change as a trial you reduce the chance that your subconscious will resist the actions related to the new belief. Tell yourself a new story and accept beliefs that will move you toward your goals.

Create a new supportive belief for a short period of time that might motivate you to take action.

You are fearless when you…

Believe in yourself

Are you holding yourself back?

A common misconception is that you need to be better than you are today or learn a bunch of new skills to be successful. The issue isn't something you need to learn, it's the belief that you aren't ready to succeed because you are missing something.

This belief – that you aren't good enough – has the opposite effect on what you are trying to achieve. You become trapped in a cycle of stress and self-doubt, trying to make yourself ready, while being distracted from realizing you already have everything you need.

Accept you are already good enough:

There is no plan you must follow or set of skills that you need to be finally labeled as successful. The only skill you need to be "better" is self-worth – believing in yourself. No amount of achievement is required, and no achievement will prove to yourself that you are enough if you don't believe it.

Tell yourself, multiple times a day, that you are enough. Convince yourself. It's up to you to learn to accept that, because nothing outside yourself will make it true.

Tell yourself, multiple times a day, that you are enough.

You are fearless when you…

Share your success

Do you overlook your success?

Winning is something we often avoid talking about. Maybe it's because we don't perceive our own success, value it, or we worry others will judge us for gloating or bragging. But if you only keep your success to yourself, no one will know, and you miss out on the benefits of people – including yourself – recognizing your achievements.

Celebrate yourself:

Start with keeping a list of your accomplishments. Personally, congratulate yourself and take a moment to feel good about what you have achieved. Then, share an accomplishment with a friend. As you get more comfortable, try sharing with a larger group. Most importantly share one of your accomplishments every day – big or small. Test this practice out for a week.

If you want to include others in this practice, try calling out the success of at least one other person each day, too. The more you share your success, the more others, and more importantly yourself, will believe in your capabilities and overall success.

Share one of your accomplishments every day – big or small.

You are fearless when you…

Create instead of chase happiness

Are you waiting to be happy?

A relentless focus on our goals can cause us to feel that nothing other than achieving them will make us happy. We forget that the things we have today were once our goals too, things we thought would make us happy.

We get stuck in a constant cycle of chasing happiness. Telling ourselves that we will finally be happy when we accomplish that next thing, overlooking that the happiness we are chasing is something we've already caught.

Remember your joy:

Think back on a goal you've already accomplished. Recall the journey from start to finish, the hard work, dedication, and the milestones you celebrated. Relive the satisfaction and sense of accomplishment you felt from making progress and finally achieving your goal. Harness the feelings.

Instead of thinking you need to achieve more to be happy, remember what you have already accomplished. Use these memories as a constant source, and a reminder, that you possess the ability to experience happiness today.

Instead of thinking you need to achieve more to be happy, remember what you have already accomplished.

You are fearless when you…

Shift from victim to creator

Are you constantly complaining?

When you are unhappy, it can be hard to focus on anything beyond that unhappiness. It becomes how you view and talk about the world, constantly highlighting the negativity, real or not, in your life.

If you constantly live in a place of negativity – in your feelings, thoughts, and beliefs – that's all you will continue to find.

Focus on what you can do:

Change your focus from what is going wrong to what you can do to make it right. Believe in the possibility that things can improve and that you are responsible for making things better.

Every issue has an opportunity. Find it. Write down what you feel is wrong and who's at fault. Now, take responsibility for the situation and figure out a solution.

When you take accountability, you also create more control over the situation and potential outcomes. Enabling you to see and create positive change from a situation where you only saw problems.

**Change your focus from what is going wrong to what you can do
to make it right.**

You are fearless when you…

Do what you want to do

How often do you "have" to do something?

Often, we feel that we have to do things because we think of them as the "good," "right," or the "responsible" thing to do. These pressures, driven by a sense of obligation or fear over what others will think, can be exhausting and breed resentment.

Accept that you are selfish:

The more honest you are with your relationships and yourself, the stronger your relationships will become. Choose to give in ways that align with your values and goals.

It's okay to say no when asked for a favor, especially when "yes" would only stem from obligation because it would be the "right" thing to do.

The people who care about you will understand and appreciate your honesty, and the people who don't, hopefully, won't stick around long enough to matter.

The more honest you are with your relationships and yourself, the stronger your relationships will become.

You are fearless when you…

Stay present

Are you often distracted?

We've all been there: doing one thing, but thinking about something else. Texting in a meeting, or thinking about a work deadline while talking to a friend.

This mental distraction often stems from being worried about the future. But, when your mind wanders, you miss out on the present moment, hindering your ability to be truly effective.

Challenge yourself to be present:

Start by setting aside 5-10 minutes each day to practice being present and prioritizing whatever you choose to focus on. Pick one thing – your breathing, music, or even a TV show – and practice focusing on just that. Put aside distractions, don't feel any pressure to make the most of the situation, and try to avoid thinking about what you are doing next.

The present moment is the only moment you can impact. Learn how to be present and spend your energy where it can be the most effective – for you and everyone else.

Put aside distractions, don't feel any pressure to make the most of the situation, and try to avoid thinking about what you are doing next.

You are fearless when you…

Focus on what's important

Are you stressed about things that won't matter?

As time progresses, we change, and so do our priorities. The things that are important to you today are probably different from what you felt was important ten years ago.

It stands to reason that the things you worry about today won't be the things you care about in the future either. Yet, we often spend time worrying about the day-to-day, forgetting that most of these concerns won't matter over time.

Reject the impact of things that won't matter:

Take a mental trip back ten years. Remember the sources of your biggest stressors: relationships, work, and specific projects. Fast forward to today. How much do those situations truly matter now? Think of the time and energy you could have saved by not investing so much emotional and physical effort back then.

Now, reflect on the most important things in your life today that consume most of your energy. Ask yourself: Will these things significantly impact your life ten years from now? Use this insight to reconsider how much time and energy you are investing in these situations and areas of your life.

The things you worry about today, won't be the things you care about in the future.

You are fearless when you…

Embrace the journey

Does it feel like progress takes "too long"?

Embarking on creating a positive change often leads to impatience. You are ready for the changes to happen "now," and want instant results.

That feeling can be a powerful source of motivation, but change takes time, and the wait may also lead to anxiety, discouragement, or even hopelessness. If it takes too long you might even start to think that it would be easier just to give up and stay the same.

Accept that what you want will take time:

Create an estimated timeline for each task you want to accomplish. Work backward from the overall goal. Be prepared to adjust your plans based on progress and unexpected events. If you aren't sure how long something will take, reflect back on different things you have accomplished in the past.

When you start feeling impatient – pause – review your timeline and tell yourself that you are on the right track. This is what you planned on happening. Remember that your timeline for progress should support you, not add stress. You are in control. If it's not working, change it.

Your timeline for progress should support you, not add stress.

You are fearless when you…

Always dream bigger

Are your goals too realistic?

Goals are influenced by your environment, upbringing, and relationships. You can limit your potential without even realizing it, sticking close to the beliefs that you've grown up with.

If your goals fit your current environment and seem possible, you may need to dream bigger.

Overestimate what you can accomplish

You are capable of so much more than you have ever been able to dream. Challenge your goals. Ask yourself: "What if I aimed ten times higher?" Write your answers down.

Repeat the question and answer it again. Spend at least 30 minutes pushing yourself to think past your initial responses.

We vastly underestimate what we are capable of, and invest too little time trying to figure out what is possible. The higher you aim, the farther you will go. Shoot for the moon. Even if you miss, you'll land among the stars.

**The higher you aim,
the farther you will go.**

You are fearless when you…

Fully commit

Are you holding yourself back?

When we aren't willing to invest all of our effort into something, it's generally due to the fact that we fear that it's the wrong decision or that we will fail.

We hesitate, doubt our abilities, and keep one foot in and one foot out of what we want to achieve, whether it's a relationship, business, or personal passion. This divided focus splits and scatters our energy, hindering any chance of success.

Commit yourself to making it work:

Identify an area in your life where you think you want to succeed but have been holding back. Set a specific time frame to fully commit. Believe: You will not let it end or fail – it has to work. Set aside your doubt. Fully invest for this period.

Pay attention to how your intention transforms and supercharges your approach, impacts the people around you, and how the world supports your focus.

The only guaranteed way to fail is to choose not to try. Decide to give yourself the chance to succeed.

**Believe: You will not let it end or fail –
it has to work.**

You are fearless when you…

Change the "how" for success

Are you ready to give up?

When you are struggling or not making progress, it's easy to start to fear that what you are doing won't work or be worth the effort. Sometimes, the issue isn't what you are working on but "how" you are trying to go about it.

If you are pushing on a "pull" door, you will never get through, but that doesn't mean the door can't work for you.

Brainstorm and experiment:

Set aside time without distractions to think strategically about the issue. Challenge yourself to come up with 5 - 10 ideas that are different from your current approach. They don't have to be right. Try to avoid judgment and keep brainstorming until an option sparks your interest. Then, try it out and see what happens. Continue the process until you create progress.

Even if an idea seems unlikely, trying something new is better than staying stuck. When you are struggling, remind yourself that anything is possible; you just need to figure out how to make it happen.

Even if an idea seems unlikely, trying something new is better than staying stuck.

You are fearless when you…

Follow your interests

Are you unsure how to change?

Change, especially something new and unfamiliar, can be daunting. Despite how much you may want to change, the uncertainty of the path ahead can feel not just uncomfortable but seemingly impossible.

There's hope though. The thing you want to achieve is more than likely something that already exists, and that means it can exist for you as well.

Immerse yourself into what you want to become:

Find where the change you want to create already exists in the world. Then, surround yourself with any related aspects to learn and make it seem more achievable: attend an event, study the topic, and create connections with people already involved and skilled in those areas.

Only when you are willing to immerse yourself in the environment you want to create will you begin to understand, and most importantly – believe – how it can be possible for you.

Immerse yourself in the environment you want to create.

You are fearless when you…

Invest in yourself

Are you avoiding personal growth?

We tend to feel most comfortable spending money on tangible "things" – the newest phone, dinner at a restaurant, or a night out, instead of the intangible, such as personal development.

The idea of investing in our own growth can be scary. We worry it might not work, strain our relationships, or alter our lives in ways we're not prepared for. However, the way we spend money reflects our investments. That means you should be spending it on what is most important to you – and most often, those aren't "things" at all.

Alter your spending habits:

Look at where you spend your money. Do the things you buy align with your values and goals? Consider spending less on "things" and investing more in areas that are important to your development, such as education, coaching, and developing skills toward your growth.

If you don't have the money to spend, remember the old saying, "Time is money." Dedicating more time, focus, and energy to those areas is another way of investing. Any small investment in yourself brings you closer to what you want, and that is a meaningful and impactful investment.

Consider spending less on "things" and investing more in areas that are important to your development.

You are fearless when you…

Ignore your critics

Do other people make you doubt yourself?

Critics are people who negatively disagree with you. They often want to convince you that you are wrong, and may try to bully you into their way of thinking.

Facing criticism can be overwhelming and discouraging, often leading to self-doubt and the urge to respond or change your opinion. However, reacting to critics would be giving them exactly what they want.

Stay true to yourself:

Critics succeed when they distract you from your goals. You may feel that you have to defend yourself, but acknowledging their negativity and their opposing views actually encourages them.

The simplest and most effective strategy to deal with critics is not to – act like they don't exist. Eventually, they may just go away, but at the very least you won't waste any energy on them.

The easiest way to deal with a critic is not to – act like they don't exist.

You are fearless when you…

Decide, don't agonize

Do you take forever to make decisions?

When you have a big decision to make, it can feel important to invest a lot of time debating pros and cons, gathering information, and consulting others. But let's be real – what you're actually doing is seeking validation for the decision you want to make – to reduce the fear that comes along with the potential decision.

Everyone has a process when it comes to making decisions. You may think it's strategic, reducing risk, or ensuring the best outcome, but generally, it just wastes time and causes stress. Imagine the time and energy you could save if you allowed yourself to make decisions without agonizing over them.

Trust your instincts:

Look at your last big decision – how long did you take to make it, and who did you consult? Learn how you make decisions, and next time try something different. Overall, you probably have a feeling about what you want to do, so why are you wasting time and energy on acting like you don't? Make a rule: only give yourself 24 hours to decide on small decisions and 48 hours for big decisions. Go with your instinct – trust yourself – and see what happens.

Make a rule: only give yourself 24 hours to decide on small decisions and 48 hours for big decisions.

You are fearless when you…

Manage your to-dos

Are you agonizing over your endless to-do list?

We all have a list of tasks or goals we intend to achieve but never actually do. The list continues to grow, and so does your fear and guilt, causing you to procrastinate even more.

Your to-do list eventually becomes a stress list that not only creates feelings of frustration and guilt but also distracts you from appreciating what you have already accomplished.

Do it or dump it:

Choose a single item from your to-do list and just do it. Stop waiting for the perfect moment. It doesn't matter what you do – or for how long – the goal is to take action. Completing even a small task creates momentum. After a few weeks, re-evaluate your list. If there are tasks you haven't even begun, remove them – no matter what. Anything you haven't started by now is just holding you back and not something you need to do. If something important was on that list, you will remember and find time for it in the future. Your to-do list should become a "do" list. Everything on your list should be something you can and will realistically "do." Without the stress from trying to do too much, you will finally feel like you've done enough.

It doesn't matter what you do – or for how long – the goal is to take action.

You are fearless when you...

Embrace your past

Are you afraid to make the same mistake?

Certain memories from our past may seem too painful to remember, leading us to avoid similar situations in the present. However, it's important to recognize that no two experiences will be the same, and just because something caused you pain in the past, doesn't mean it will cause you pain today.

Grow through reflection:

Painful memories are not reasons to avoid new experiences; rather, they are lessons for making different choices in the future. For instance, a toxic relationship in your past is not a sign to avoid all relationships. Instead, it offers insights on how to select a partner and manage a relationship.

Take the time to review areas of your life that you've been avoiding due to the fear of repeating past mistakes. Pick one that you would deem less risky, and adopt the belief that the outcome can be different by applying what you've learned from your past experiences. Now, face your past and create a new experience. Often we get caught up in the fear of repeating our past, but the world didn't end when you had a painful experience before – it won't this time either.

Painful memories in your life are not reasons to avoid experiences, they are lessons on how to do something different the next time you face a similar situation.

You are fearless when you…

Ask for help

Are you waiting for someone to help you?

Many people are afraid to ask for help, even when they know what they need and who can assist them. There's a variety of beliefs that tend to hold them back: assuming others would help if they wanted to, feeling undeserving or unprepared for the help, or the perception that asking for help is a sign of weakness. As a result, despite their desire and need for help, they don't try to find or ask for it.

Find the support you need:

Accept a new belief: Many people in the world want to help you, but you have to give them the opportunity and ask. Reach out to people you know who have succeeded in your areas of interest. Even those you barely know might be willing to talk with you and provide direction.

The more people you ask, the greater chance you have of making a connection. Every "no" is the same as not asking, but every "yes" from someone is a door to new opportunities. Remember, if someone agrees to help you, they genuinely want to, and those are the people that you want in your life.

Many people in the world want to help you, but you have to give them the opportunity and ask.

You are fearless when you…

Invest in community

Are you too busy to make time for friends?

Many things may seem more urgent than socializing, but building a community can bring you more wealth than any other type of work.

Relationships are the global currency of life. Their value cannot be purchased with money and is impossible to quantify. Yet, the benefits will continue to pay out for far longer than anything else.

Connect with someone every day:

Reach out to one person each day – not to make plans – simply to say hello or share something they might appreciate. Every time you connect, you strengthen that relationship.

Imagine that every touch point is a percent point of growth, just like in other financial investments. With consistency, these relationships compound, turn into a community, and that value is priceless.

Reach out to one person each day – not to make plans – just to say hello or share something they might appreciate.

You are fearless when you…

Never rush a hug

Are you ignoring your relationships?

When you are in a state of worry or stress about everything you have to do, it's easy to rush or have less patience for the people closest to you.

Your relationships don't have project deadlines or time limits, so they may not seem as important when something "needs" to get done. But, in the long run, when you do this, you miss out on the benefits of connecting and could cause people to think you don't care.

Nothing should be more important than the people you care about, especially when they're in front of you.

Pause and connect in person:

It doesn't matter how rushed you feel, if someone is in front of you, give them your full attention. More specifically, there is always time to put down whatever you are working on and give the person a hug.

Take advantage of the moments you have with the people that are important to you, at some point, those moments may not exist, and then you will wish you had more time.

Take advantage of the moments you have with the people that are important to you.

You are fearless when you…

Watch your words

Are you "just joking" more often than not?

We often use sarcasm and negativity as an attempt to connect with our relationships or deal with an uncomfortable situation.

Saying hurtful things, even through the frame of "just joking" will likely lead to people in your life who are not telling you how much what you say hurts them.

Be aware of what you say and how you say it:

For one day, challenge yourself to not say anything negative. Pay attention to when you are tempted to be negative – do you notice it more with certain people, in specific places, or at certain times? If you notice any trends, adjust your environment or mindset to reduce the negativity.

Additionally, for a further challenge, make an effort to use words that are more positive and uplifting.

We tend to be more careless around those closest to us; if you are wondering how to start, try incorporating less negativity in conversation with those people first.

For one day, challenge yourself to not say anything negative.

You are fearless when you…

Care how you treat others

Do you act differently when you are in a bad mood?

When we don't feel like our best selves – rough days, bad moods, exhaustion – it can impact our behavior, including how we treat others.

These emotions can be overwhelming, causing us to forget how we want to show up for our relationships. However, if you care about treating others in the way they deserve, it's important to find a way to get out of your own head.

Treat everyone like it's their birthday:

Imagine that everyone you interact with is celebrating their birthday. It's their special day, and you couldn't even imagine making it a negative one.

Right away, your feelings and thoughts are positive and attuned to the other person – not what's going on with you. This practice not only enhances your mood but encourages others to be positive too.

The more you do this, the more others will pick up on it, feel you are celebrating them, and become more positive when they are with you.

Imagine that everyone you interact with is celebrating their birthday.

You are fearless when you…

Have the hard conversations

Are you avoiding certain people?

Communication is the key to solving conflict and healing relationships, but we rarely try to proactively communicate with people we aren't getting along with. You might be afraid and worry about what will happen if you have a conversation with someone that you are having issues with, but you already know what will happen if you don't. Without the right channels of communication, these issues will never stop getting in your way, things may get worse, and the people will always be sources of conflict.

Create opportunities for conversation:

Stop viewing the other person as an enemy who causes problems and start seeing them as a partner in creating solutions. When you can transition from approaching the conflict as a fight to win, and instead view it as a problem to solve, you will be able to heal the relationship. Pick a person you tend to have a lot of conflict with, and set up a conversation now, before your next conflict. When you approach the person without being in a fight, you have the opportunity to have a different type of conversation.

Remember that every person you have a conflict with is likely someone that you would rather not have conflict with. So choose to create other types of conversations with them.

Stop viewing the other person as an enemy who causes problems and start seeing them as a partner in creating solutions.

You are fearless when you…

Reconnect to what motivates you

Are you overwhelmed and unmotivated?

In the hustle of daily life, it's all too easy to overwork yourself. The fear of missing out or the anxiety of making mistakes can deprioritize the things you actually care about.

Even doing things you enjoy can leave you drained if all you can think about is your next to-do or deadline. While motivation and a sense of meaning can seem out of reach during these times – they are always there if you choose to look. Often, when you feel overwhelmed, you forget that the reasons that motivate you are still inside you.

Remember your "why":

You can find your motivation at any time by connecting to the meaning and greater impact of the things you spend time on. Dedicate a time without distractions to reflect and reconnect to the deeper purpose and impact of your efforts. The day-to-day is "what" you do, but the "what" isn't the thing that will sustain your interest. You need to remember the "why" at the core of your actions. Write it down, and spend time sharing it with others. Your "why" can be a never-ending source of energy and motivation if you can remember that it exists.

You can find your motivation at any time by connecting to the meaning behind the things you spend time on.

You are fearless when you…

Embrace never doing "enough"

Do you always feel like you aren't doing "enough"?

When you feel a sense of purpose and meaning from what you do, you will always feel driven to "do more" – and that you haven't "done enough."

That feeling of always wanting to do more comes from having something in your life that gives you purpose. It's what motivates you. Although the feeling can be uncomfortable, it's actually a gift at the core of your success.

Accept the discomfort:

Having a purpose means you will never be completely satisfied. It's up to you to accept that you've done enough. Rest and celebrate your successes – even when you don't feel entirely successful. You can always do more later.

The beauty of having a purpose is that it will never be fulfilled. It's supposed to be an ongoing journey. While you may never fully achieve it, the fulfillment it creates along the way is what truly matters.

It's up to you to accept when
you've done enough.

You are fearless when you…

Experience wonder wherever you are

Do you get bored with life?

Getting caught up in our daily tasks, worries, and fears can make us lose sight of the wonder that surrounds us. We often overlook the uniqueness and preciousness of life when overwhelmed. Yet, no matter where you are or what you are doing, there is always wonder that can go along with it.

Be amazed at the world we live in:

Take a moment to observe your surroundings and choose an object to focus on. Consider its origins: where did it come from, and how many individuals played a part in bringing it to you? Take the food you eat for instance – it started as a seed, grew into produce, and passed through countless hands before reaching your plate.

If that isn't enough to leave you in awe, zoom out and broaden your perspective. Recognize your existence for what it is, a mere speck of cosmic stardust in a universe of universes.

Engaging in this practice of heightened awareness and reflection can awaken feelings of joy, happiness, meaning, and gratitude. Remind yourself the world is magical, and you get to be in it.

Remind yourself the world is magical, and you get to be in it.

You are fearless when you…

Create your purpose

Are you trying to "find" your purpose?

Before I became fearless, I lived based on what I thought was a simple piece of advice: find your purpose. Not only was the process of "searching for meaning" a constant drain on my mental health, but that idea was wrong and misleading. Your purpose is a feeling, and feelings come from within you – it's not something you find, nor is it something that anyone can give to you; it's something you can choose to create.

Identify and pursue what is meaningful:

Start by identifying the things that are most meaningful to you. Pick one and give yourself permission to focus on it for the time being. You can always change your mind.

Experiment and have experiences with your chosen direction. For example, read a recent article, go to a related event, or ask someone in the field to talk – as you have more experiences you will start to shape your purpose. Does it feel right? If not, try something else. Your purpose is something you cultivate over time – through intention and experiences – it's always going to be there, you don't need to find it. Just give yourself a chance to create it.

Your purpose is a feeling, and feelings
come from within you – it's not
something you find, nor is it something
that anyone can give to you;
it's something you can
choose to create.

As an additional resource for taking action and working on each tip, download the **Becoming** app.
liveforyourselfconsulting.com/becomingfearless

Professional

You are fearless when you…

Remember how great you are

Do you struggle with feeling like a "fraud" at work?

It's understandable that you occasionally worry you aren't "good enough." But lacking confidence in your skills and abilities doesn't just hold you back, it can keep you from getting ahead. These feelings will stop you from speaking up, asking for what you want, and forming positive relationships – but only if you let them. Doubt doesn't have to control you and what you do.

Remember your previous success:

When you have trouble believing in yourself, remember that you earned the role you have. You were hired because others already believe in you, now you just have to learn to believe in yourself.

Be your greatest champion. Reflect on and make a list of your achievements, accolades, and other recognitions you've received at work. Take this information and create a success folder on your desktop or in your email. Review it when you need to cheer yourself on.

It's also helpful to post something you are proud of where you can see it every day. When you are constantly reminded of your successes and skills, you will be more likely to believe you deserve them.

Be your greatest champion.

You are fearless when you…

Accept the true meaning of work

Are you making work your entire life?

No matter how passionate and energized you feel by the work that you do, if you are always working on it, you are doing something wrong. Think about what you are truly working for – it's not to be able to work more.

We ultimately work to pay for the life we want to experience, but oftentimes get lost in the stress and anxiety of "protecting" our jobs, or the discomfort of trying to figure out what else to spend our free time on. If all you do is work, then your priorities aren't in alignment with what work is truly for: to create a life that fulfills you.

Make time for life outside of work:

The only way you are going to get used to not working is to create more times when you aren't working. Consider the times you are working outside of "typical" work hours and cut out 1-2 times each week that you usually work off-hours: going in early, staying late, working on the weekends. Another way to work less is to make plans that require you to leave: scheduling a weekly lunch or dinner with a friend or taking a class in the evening. Remember, work isn't something that can replace or sustain your life – that's why it's called "working" and not called "living."

The only way you are going to get used to not working is to create more times when you aren't working.

You are fearless when you…

Avoid burning out

Are you doing everything?

If you are working in an environment that constantly stresses you out, you are probably overworked, exhausted, and on the verge of burning out. When your energy is constantly drained, you are probably doing more than you need to, while being afraid that you are still not doing enough.

Do less:

Hit the reset button on how you approach your job. Treat your job as if it's brand new. Imagine you just got hired at the same position and start work tomorrow. Your first task is to work with your manager to create your onboarding plan. What are your top priorities? What work do you stop, start, and continue doing?

Overall, professionals who have learned how to avoid burnout keep their plates 75% full. They know how to prioritize work based on a healthy limit, focus on what's most important, delegate, and say no or not yet to work.

The right balance keeps you engaged, occasionally busy, but always able to manage the work. It's more important to avoid burnout, and prioritize yourself than to meet any projection or goal.

Prioritize work based on a healthy limit, focus on what's most important, delegate, and say no or not yet to work.

You are fearless when you…

Never have "too much" work

Are you constantly stressed about work?

Even when we are not at work, we often continue to give our time to it, worrying about "all the work we have to do." That fear doesn't do anything to help you – worrying doesn't get work done – it just allows work to take up even more of your valuable time.

Let go of work until it's time:

Spending time worrying – about anything – won't make it go faster or better. Take control of your anxieties and set clear boundaries for when you will and will not work – including time thinking about your work.

Make a detailed work plan for when you will complete the work, get your worries out of your mind and on paper, and schedule time in your calendar for when you are not going to spend time working – "no-work time."

When you start worrying about work, redirect your thoughts and remind yourself, there's nothing else you can work on at the moment. Work will still be there to do when it's time.

When you start worrying about work, redirect your thoughts and remind yourself, there's nothing else you can work on at the moment.

You are fearless when you…

Clarify expectations

Are you struggling to feel successful?

Many people believe that career advancement will make them feel more confident and successful. However, it's not uncommon for people to find themselves struggling even more with self-doubt once they move up in their careers. They worry that with more power comes more responsibility, and the greater chance of failure or disappointment – which doesn't have to be true.

Define what you are responsible for:

It's important to maintain perspective as you take on a more senior role. You may have more responsibility but you aren't responsible for everything. The things that defined your success before, are not what you are responsible for now. Work with your manager to define the scope of your role, goals for the position, and quantifiable metrics and key objectives. Get specific on your priorities. Share your progress and leverage your manager to problem-solve when needed. As you create more clarity in regards to the expectations for your role, focus on what you are actually responsible for – the areas you defined with your manager – and let go of the things you aren't. Not only will you feel more successful, but your manager will believe you are, which is important for your continued success.

Work with your manager to define the scope of your role, goals for the position, quantifiable metrics and key objectives.

You are fearless when you…

Create the job you want at the job you have

Do you wish you could improve your current job?

When we're ready for a new job, we often assume that it will have to be with a new company. The idea of starting over can seem like a fresh start and a solution to all the things that bother you about your current job. However, there is no guarantee that a new job will be an improvement. It might seem easier to leave than to try and fix the issues, but if you are considering quitting, then you have nothing to lose by trying to fix where you are.

Look for opportunity where you are:

When you know you want to leave your job, you should also know the reasons why you want to leave: the actual work you do, the workload, who you work with, compensation, and maybe even how your manager treats you. This is the information you need to share with your manager to try and find a solution. Schedule a meeting with your leader to discuss the areas you would want to change. Treat the conversation as a problem to solve instead of things to complain about. Work together and avoid making demands but don't hold back from asking for what would make you happy. You might be surprised what you get when you try. Also, the worst thing that can happen is you do exactly what you were going to do in the first place and find a new job.

If you are considering quitting, then you have nothing to lose by trying to fix where you are.

You are fearless when you…

Control your job satisfaction

Do you want to be happier at work?

How you feel towards your work often changes as time goes on. You may become bored, stop liking certain coworkers, or lose touch with the aspects that made you feel like you were making an impact.

It's easier to blame your employer, leader, or job than yourself, but creating and sustaining the connection to your work is up to you. You just have to take responsibility for your levels of job satisfaction.

Work the way you want to:

It's up to you to craft a way of working that enables you to find joy and fulfillment in whatever you do. Crafting your job, and job satisfaction is generally connected to three main categories; changing your work – focusing more on what you enjoy doing and less on what you don't, social connections – who you choose to engage with, and reconnecting to the meaning of your work – the way you perceive your impact.

If you start to feel disconnected from your work, reflect on how you can improve each of the three areas. You can craft your own job satisfaction. Happiness with your work is not a given, but it is something you can create.

Job satisfaction is generally connected to three main categories; changing your work, social connections, and reconnecting to the meaning of your work.

You are fearless when you…

Take pride in your work

Does every workday feel like checking a box?

If you go to work with a "check the box" mentality, it's impossible to feel good about what you do. When you don't care about your work, it can be difficult and even nerve-wracking to invest any more time or energy into your job. You know it's a waste of time, and you eventually start to feel as if you are missing out on your career and life.

Impress yourself:

If you are choosing to stay at your job and want to be happy, you have to give yourself a reason to care about the work. The more you invest in your job, the more you will feel it's worthwhile.

Choose to show up and engage in your work for one day. Give it your full attention, and leverage your skills, expertise, and energy. Be proud of your work.

When you are shutting down work for the day, take a moment to reflect on your accomplishments. Recognize the differences you've made in the world and the unique professional strengths you used to make an impact.

You have to give yourself a reason to care about the work.

You are fearless when you…

Choose the meetings you attend

Do meetings always feel like a waste of your time?

Unneeded meetings are the biggest drain on time and the largest source of frustration in many organizations. Despite this, many professionals are afraid and hesitate to turn down meeting invitations, even when they believe they don't need to attend. They are often worried about offending the organizer, missing out on important information, or feeling like others will judge them.

Imagine how much more productive and efficient your workday could be if you only attended meetings that truly helped you succeed in your job.

Say no to ineffective meetings:

It's your job to make sure you are only in meetings that are valuable for you. Prior to automatically accepting a meeting, question if you truly need to attend. Can it be delegated to someone else on your team, addressed in an email, or with a direct follow-up message? Now, do the same process for meetings that are already on your calendar. If you need to attend, ask for an agenda ahead of time and take 10 - 15 minutes before the meeting to plan on what you hope to share and learn. Meetings are time, and your time is valuable, so treat them that way.

It's your job to make sure you are only in meetings that are valuable for you.

You are fearless when you…

Engage in meetings

Do you avoid engaging in meetings?

Many people miss out on taking advantage of the meetings they attend. They hesitate to share their opinions for fear of judgment, feel it's not their role or place to speak up, or have so much work to do that they use it as extra time to get other work done. But how you engage in meetings greatly affects how others perceive you at work.

Your colleagues, and even more importantly your leaders, can tell -- and will judge you -- if you aren't paying attention or contributing.

Highlight your value in meetings:

When you are in a meeting, that is your best and often only opportunity to show your capabilities and personality to others outside of your actual work. It is your chance to be on stage, in the spotlight, and be more visible to anyone who's in attendance. Ask questions. Share opinions. Call on others to do the same. Set a rule to at least share one idea and question in every meeting. Utilize meeting times to demonstrate that you are engaged, care about the organization, and skilled at what you do. This helps grow your professional presence and build credibility with others.

Utilize meeting times to demonstrate that you are engaged, care about the organization, and skilled at what you do.

You are fearless when you…

Trust first

Do you have a hard time trusting others?

Trust is a critical component of a positive and enjoyable work environment. It creates a feeling of safety and leads to more direct communication, positive relationships, greater innovation, and productivity.

It can feel scary to trust others at work, especially if you aren't sure if they trust you, or if someone broke your trust in the past. However, trust is incredibly important to your professional reputation, and ultimately your success if you have to work with anyone other than yourself.

Cultivate aspects of trust:

You can build trust with others in several ways, but the most important action is to give trust first. It's easier to trust than to constantly be skeptical of others, and giving trust creates a dynamic where the other person feels trust toward you. Some examples of trusting others include: supporting their work, admitting when you are wrong, communicating directly, and giving the benefit of the doubt.

You need to be able to trust the people you work with, and the best place to start is by giving them a reason to trust you.

Giving trust creates a dynamic where the other person feels trust towards you.

You are fearless when you…

Respect the way others work

Do you feel your way is the right way?

It can be stressful to accept someone's work when you know a different way, or in your mind, a better way, to get it done. The process that works for you might feel ideal, but trying to impose that on others only gets in their way.

Every person you work with has their own way of doing things. If it doesn't impact the ultimate outcome of their work, trying to change or control their process will be perceived as overstepping and disrespectful.

Support but stay out of the process:

People who are given the autonomy to complete their work believe they are more in control, engaged, and satisfied overall. The moment you try to get in their way is the moment they perceive you as someone who isn't supportive. Focus on the final product, not the process. If you are held accountable for the work, set up check-in meetings to assess progress, but let them use their strengths and skills to get to the final product. It's okay to offer suggestions for efficiency and time management but keep out of their method of getting the work done to ensure that your co-workers see you as a positive relationship and want to continue working with you.

Focus on the final product, not the process.

You are fearless when you…

Ask questions before making suggestions

Are you always trying to solve others' problems?

When someone approaches you with an issue, it's natural to feel compelled to help them solve it. Often the instinct to offer advice or solutions comes from the fear that if someone needs your help and you don't provide a solution, you're letting them down, or might seem incompetent. However, being quick to problem-solve can lead to more problems. Offering solutions too soon might not only lead to incorrect advice but also prevent the other person from working through the issue on their own and developing a more personalized solution.

Listen and ask questions:

When you are approached with a problem, listen and resist the urge to give feedback right away. Instead, ask the other person what they need. Do they just want to be heard, brainstorm, or do they want to problem solve? If they are looking for advice, a question can be more powerful and effective than any answer. Asking questions will provide you with more specific information, and give the other person a chance to learn and solve their own problem. When someone comes to you with an issue, focus on the opportunity to learn more about the problem and strengthen the relationship. You will be helping them more than just "solving" their problem.

A question can be more powerful and effective than any answer.

You are fearless when you…

Lead with optimism

How do you respond when others complain?

Maintaining a positive attitude at work can be challenging, especially when it involves other people complaining. Aligning with others' negative views can be a way to strengthen relationships, but it creates a dilemma between trying to stay positive and the need to fit in. However, for those aspiring to grow professionally, negativity can tarnish your reputation and prevent an opportunity to motivate others towards greater organizational goals.

Always find the positive:

If you want to grow in your career, it's on you to be the voice of optimism. If you notice a problem, encourage finding a solution. If others are complaining, you can empathize, while still pointing out more positive aspects.

The people that others want to work with and trust are champions of their organization and the people in it. If you are bright when others cast shadows, you will be the one who stands out, and others will take notice.

The people that others want to work
with and trust are champions of their
organization and the people in it.

You are fearless when you...

Focus on solutions

Are you trying to help by highlighting problems?

It may seem like common sense to approach the people in charge with issues that you discover. We think they are responsible for finding solutions, but they aren't the only ones who can solve them – you can.

You may think that it's outside your scope of work or worried about speaking up, but no matter how well-intentioned or important, people don't want more problems.

Share a solution if you call attention to a problem:

If you can identify a problem, you can likely find a solution, or at least try to come up with an idea. Take that extra step when you find a problem: treat it like it's your responsibility and something you have to solve.

By adopting this mindset and strategy, you will not only impress your manager, but also establish a reputation as someone who can identify issues, solve problems, and go above and beyond for the organization.

**Take that extra step when you find
a problem: treat it like it's
your responsibility.**

You are fearless when you…

Stay focused

Are you constantly multi-tasking?

In fast-paced work environments with overflowing to-do lists, there's a constant temptation to multitask in order to get more done. You don't want to disappoint anyone, so you try to do everything. Multi-tasking not only increases the likelihood of errors, but it also makes it impossible to function at your best. Rather than saving time, it splits your focus, reduces the quality of your work, and creates even more stress, leading to a cycle of anxiety and potential consequences at work.

Focus on one task at a time:

We try to do more than one thing at a time because we aren't sure which tasks are more important. All tasks are not equally critical. Prioritize your to-do list. Rank the items by their level of importance and deadlines. Commit to only working on one task until it is completed. Help yourself prevent multi-tasking by minimizing distractions: turn off notifications, close browsers, and email, and work somewhere more private. This ensures that the task not only gets done, but it gets your undivided attention and best effort. By doing so, you will transform your productivity, allowing yourself to achieve more in less time, and finally feel productive yourself.

Commit to only working on one task until it is completed.

You are fearless when you…

Give feedback

Do you avoid giving feedback?

People generally avoid giving feedback because they are afraid of doing it wrong or offending someone. It can seem easier to not give feedback, so why risk it, even if all it's doing is complimenting and empowering someone.

Feedback is a conversational tool that can build and strengthen your relationships. Not only does it help others grow, but it can also improve work outcomes. When you keep feedback to yourself, you are doing everyone a disservice.

Put feedback into practice:

Start looking for opportunities to give feedback – be specific, discuss the impact of the behavior, and ask the other person for their thoughts or solutions. If you are uncomfortable providing constructive feedback, start with positive feedback – focus on the highlight reel – the top plays from people around you.

If you take the first step to becoming comfortable with providing feedback, you can create a more open and honest dialogue in your relationships with your coworkers. You'll gain their respect, and they'll probably start giving you feedback, too.

Start looking for opportunities to give feedback – be specific, discuss the impact of the behavior, and ask the other person for their thoughts or solutions.

You are fearless when you…

Solicit feedback

Do you wonder how people perceive you at work?

Often at work, we doubt ourselves and wonder what our colleagues and managers think about our performance. However, the fear of asking for feedback can make us too uncomfortable and nervous to ask. Without taking the initiative to find out though, we will never know, at least not until a performance review or possible layoff.

Make it part of the conversation:

If you want feedback, ask for it. Be specific, let the person know you will listen openly and without judgment, and make sure to ask at a time that's as close to the situation as you want feedback from. For example, "I'm trying to improve my presentation skills. Can you share something you thought went great, and something I can do even better? I won't be offended by anything you say and I'm really curious about your opinion."

When you receive feedback it's important not to argue or defend yourself. Instead, be curious and ask questions to learn more. If you show your coworkers that you are open to feedback, you are more likely to receive it.

If you want feedback, ask for it.

You are fearless when you…

Delegate

Are you involved in everything?

It's common to be worried about work getting done right. If it's wrong, it might reflect poorly on you, and so you try and manage any work you are involved in to the smallest detail. Even if you are not the one doing the work. This is not only impossible, it's inefficient, and will lead to more mistakes and higher levels of stress, for you and everyone you are trying to micromanage. If you are often overwhelmed with work or told that you are "too focused on the details" you probably should be delegating some of your responsibilities to others.

Categorize your work and then let go:

Your job isn't to do all the work yourself, it's to ensure that everyone else is getting done what they need to do. To feel more comfortable with giving away "your" work, you can categorize the tasks into the ones that are more or less critical to the organization, and adjust your level of oversight based on the impact not doing the task correctly will have. More important tasks might need you to do the work with someone, while you may just need to know that less important tasks were completed. Ideally, delegate work that others can perform at least 80% as effectively as you could. Letting go of your work can feel scary, but it's not your work, it's just work that needs to get done.

Your job isn't to do all the work
yourself, it's to ensure that everyone
else is getting done what
they need to do.

You are fearless when you

Understand your audience

Do you overshare information?

When we need to communicate updates at work it's not uncommon to fear that people won't understand us unless we share enough details, or worse, they might think less of you without the right context. This concern and fear drive us to overshare, and although we intend to improve clarity and avoid misunderstandings, the result is often counterproductive. Excessive information can overwhelm your audience, create confusion, and reflect poorly on your communication skills.

Communicate the most important information:

The value of your communication is often equal to how much you prepare. Take the time before sharing information to reflect on the areas your audience cares about and align your message to their needs. Share your main point, the reasons for your audience to care, and the actions you need them to take.

If you need to provide more details it's best to provide them as an attachment so they don't interfere with your main points. Communication is pointless if people don't listen to you or understand what you are sharing. When in doubt, be brief, and then check on comprehension from your audience.

Share your main point, the reasons for your audience to care, and the actions you need them to take.

You are fearless when you…

Show up as an executive

Do you want a seat at the table?

Your professional presence influences not only how others perceive and respond to you but also your future career opportunities. Many of us do what our jobs require, and nothing else. But that means you are limiting your behavior and attitude to the level you are at in the organization, and not acting like, and most likely not being treated like, an executive.

Mirror the executives in your organization:

If you want to be included in strategic discussions and treated like an executive, then you are going to have to start acting like one. Pay attention to the leaders around you: what they wear, how they talk, and the way they treat others – these elements contribute to their executive presence. Pick one new behavior and try it out.

You may feel nervous acting beyond the "limitations" of your role, but your engagement, presence, and attitude are not limited by your job title. You have a choice to adopt the characteristics of the executives in your organization and be seen as a natural candidate for leadership discussions and future roles.

If you want to be included in strategic discussions and treated like an executive, then you are going to have to start acting like one.

You are fearless when you…

Take action towards career clarity

Are you wondering what's next for your career?

People often get stuck when they don't have a clear plan for what they want to do next for their career. They are afraid that if they take action they might make the wrong choice or miss out on a better opportunity. They are trying to maximize the next decision so end up doing nothing. But by not making any decision, they are limiting all possibilities.

Get curious:

The only way to make a decision when you are stuck is to get curious and make a decision. You can always make another decision afterward.

Pick one option you want to explore and identify something you can do to test it out. Possibly a conversation with someone in the field, or a related volunteer role. Exploring might seem scary, but you are not changing your life, you are just getting curious through action.

Every new experience creates more information, which makes the next choice even more informed, and so forth. When you lead with curiosity, you are leading yourself to clarity.

The only way to make a decision when you are stuck, is to get curious and make a decision.

You are fearless when you…

Give yourself permission

Are you waiting to be told to take initiative?

Many of us fall into the trap of waiting for permission before taking action in our careers. We might want to be proactive – apply to that promotion, ask to be in that crucial meeting, or seek mentorship from more senior leaders – but are afraid of overstepping, or making a mistake.

This concern holds us back, making us passive and reactive, only responding to opportunities that come our way. As a result, we risk missing out on shaping our career path and creating more control of our professional growth.

Hold yourself accountable:

Your career is your responsibility. You don't need permission to start a project, learn a new skill, or go for a promotion.

Reflect on the areas of your career where you could assert more control and accountability. What steps can you take right now to move closer to achieving the things you want?

Choose an action that will take you one step closer to your goals, and you will have taken back ownership of your career.

Your career is your responsibility.

You are fearless when you…

Lead your manager

Are you waiting for your manager to follow through?

Initiating a conversation with your manager about your needs or goals is a significant and courageous step. However, it's important to remember that your manager has a lot of other responsibilities.

While they are there to support you, your needs may not always be at the top of their list. If something you've discussed isn't happening, then you are still responsible for making sure it does.

Hold your manager accountable:

When you need something from your manager, it's up to you to make sure it happens. This means you need to follow up.

Be proactive yet polite. Keep a record of your conversations and regularly update your manager on progress during your one-on-ones. Most importantly, make it easy for your manager to help you by reminding them – maybe even multiple times.

Remember, it's not their fault if they don't follow up; if you haven't taken the responsibility to ensure they do.

When you need something from your manager, it's up to you to make sure it happens.

You are fearless when you…

Elevate your performance

Are you waiting to prove your worth?

If you are excelling in your current role, you may expect that you will be offered a promotion. You've been working hard, putting in the hours, and getting your work done.

But being good at your job is rarely enough to convince employers that you should be raised to the next level. If you limit yourself to what you are expected to do, no one will be able to see your full potential.

Act as if you have already been promoted:

If you want a promotion, you have to act as if you already have the role. Hold yourself to the standards of the new position, leveling up your work, and campaigning to make sure others know about it. Prove that you already have the skills and you'll be known as the right fit when a position becomes available.

Be patient and prepared to work at this for 6-12 months before you see any impact, and make sure your manager knows that you want a promotion early on in the process.

If you want a promotion, you have to act as if you already have the role.

You are fearless when you…

Increase your visibility

Are you working in a silo?

It takes more than hard work to progress in your career, especially if no one knows what you are doing. You may hesitate to share your work and achievements due to feeling like you are bragging, or you might think promoting your work is your manager's responsibility. However, if you want to progress in your career, it is important that others know who you are and the impact you have on the organization.

Make sure everyone knows what you do:

Proactively increase your visibility and network in your organization. Engage with coworkers, specifically those one or two levels above you, and highlight your projects and achievements. Identify opportunities to present your work in meetings and increase your participation in group discussions. It's critical that senior leaders understand how your work has impacted their success, and your peers are aware of your responsibilities and achievements.

Being recognized by those in positions that can offer you growth opportunities is key. Internal networking doesn't have to be a full-time job, aim for just enough effort so that people know your strengths and that you exist.

Proactively increase your visibility and network in your organization.

You are fearless when you…

Stay current on your career opportunities

Are you aware of what your skills are worth?

The job market is constantly changing, from compensation and skill requirements to job titles. Knowing your worth – outside of your current job – is vital to understanding and navigating your most successful career path. It may feel wrong to look for a new job when you aren't interested in a move, or you may be nervous that your employer will find out. However, the only way you will know what's happening in the job market, and learn more about your future career options, is to spend time looking.

Apply and interview often:

The best way to know what's out there and what you are worth is to meet with potential employers. Not only will you learn what opportunities are available, but you will also have the opportunity to practice telling stories about your professional experiences.

Prior to the search, make sure your resume and LinkedIn profile are up to date. Also, you should be able to clearly communicate the projects you've worked on that best highlight your skills. Each conversation will help you learn more about the job market, practice honing your "pitch," and highlight available career opportunities.

The best way to know what's out there and what you are worth is to meet with potential employers.

You are fearless when you…

Build your brand

Are you only focusing on your current job?

It's easy to allow yourself to be defined by what you do and where you work. People often feel afraid to try out anything new or obligated to focus on their current company and role. But your career – your brand – is greater than any one role. Once you leave your current job, your organization is only part of your career story.

Explore opportunities outside of your organization:

Define your long-term professional goals. Reflect on the experiences you want to have by the time you retire, the projects you want to have been a part of, the people you aim to collaborate with, and the impact you want to leave behind. What do you want your legacy to be?

Then, determine what you can or need to do now – apart from your current role – to support your career goals. Engage in activities that contribute to your career brand: join associations, contribute to research publications, participate in podcasts, write articles, or even start a side business. Pick one thing that's more than just your job, and take a proactive step in the direction of your future career.

Determine what you can or need to do now – apart from your current role – to support your career goals.

You are fearless when you…

Become memorable at events

Are you getting lost in the crowd?

All too often, we will make the effort to attend an event expecting to network but spend most of the time either talking to no one or to the wrong people. It can be uncomfortable and feel awkward to proactively meet people at an event, but many people there are in a similar mindset.

Make the effort to stand out:

To ensure you get noticed at events, introduce yourself to anyone who seems to be directing others or working the room. These individuals are typically event organizers or event regulars, are extra welcoming, and can facilitate introductions to others. Also, don't hesitate to approach other people. Even a few minutes of talking to someone one-on-one establishes an initial connection that opens the door for further conversation.

Another tip for standing out is to attend events at times when there will likely be lower attendance – such as holidays, during bad weather, or when competing events are scheduled. Attending an event when people have reasons not, to helps you stand out and increases your chance of creating a lasting impression. If you are going to an event, you might as well make it useful, and invest the energy to make an impact and be remembered.

If you are going to an event, you might as well make it useful, and invest the energy to make an impact and be remembered.

You are fearless when you…

Do the work after you network

Are you meeting people but not keeping in touch?

While taking the time to network and make initial connections offers potential value, these connections do nothing for you if you don't do the work to turn them into relationships.

You might feel uncomfortable following up or be afraid of seeming too forward, but it doesn't take long for you to become a stranger to them again if you don't reach out.

Invest in creating a relationship:

Next time you make new contacts, commit to following up immediately. If you are feeling insecure or nervous about reaching out or aren't sure what to say, consider whether the potential for the new relationship outweighs the risk. Focus on the benefits of the connection instead of the fears and doubts.

The longer you hesitate, the less likely the contacts will remember you. Keep in mind, people generally don't spend their time on things that don't interest them. So, if someone was willing to connect with you, they did so because they wanted to – and they are likely waiting for your follow-up.

Next time you make new contacts, commit to following up immediately.

You are fearless when you…

Prepare multiple paths

Are you waiting for that one thing to work out?

When we finally set our sights on a goal, it's easy to believe – and fear – that there's only one path to success. But this can lead to unnecessary stress and cause you to miss out on paths that will lead to greater success. Everything you want to achieve has a multitude of paths to get there. The more you limit your options, the less of a chance you will have to actually achieve your goal. For example, if you become hyper-focused on getting a specific job, you might turn down other connections or unexpected experiences that could eventually lead you to your dream role.

Explore other paths toward your goal:

Plan more strategically and long-term. Your next action doesn't have to lead directly to your goal, but it should eventually get there. Instead of just focusing on a specific job or company, build relationships in the industry overall. Become involved in professional organizations, attend networking events, or reach out to specific individuals at companies you are interested in working at. Often, we think that if one thing doesn't work out, it means that we have failed. But there is never only one way to accomplish your goal, especially when you create multiple paths to get there.

The more you limit your options, the less of a chance you will have to actually achieve your goal.

You are fearless when you…

Secure your financial future

Are you worried about losing your job?

If you are afraid of the financial implications of not having your current job, then it might be time to get creative and find other opportunities to utilize your skills and expertise. The conventional 40-hour work week isn't the only way there is to work, and it can limit you financially and professionally.

Earn multiple streams of income:

You are selling your skills to your current employer for a specific job. They don't own your expertise – you do. In order to create other sources of income, you need to expand who you are leveraging your skills for.

Creating another income stream, part-time, contract, or even full-time are all possibilities. Explore freelancing, consulting, or launching a side business. If possible, identify work that will benefit your broader career, so you are also gaining valuable experience and professional development.

It will take time, but by leveraging your skills to create multiple income streams, you'll gain financial security and become more confident and empowered throughout your career.

In order to create other sources of income, you need to expand who you are leveraging your skills for.

Final thoughts

You deserve to be fearless.

Get curious about your fears.

Feel your feelings. Think about your thoughts. Challenge – don't automatically believe – your beliefs. Then, take action.

Remember, the choice is always yours. Fear isn't in control. It's just information. Use it to serve you.

Choose to become fearless.

About the author: Benjamin Ritter, EdD, MBA, MPH

Dr. Benjamin Ritter has made it his mission to guide and empower others to become confident leaders in their lives and careers. Driven by the belief that every person deserves to "live for themselves," Ben founded  *Live for Yourself Consulting* and has grown it into a global brand where he gets to do what he loves most: help highly driven professionals figure out what's holding them back, enabling them to become fearless and take accountability and feel empowered to create a life that they love.

He's coached over 500 leaders one-on-one and worked with over 10,000 through workshops at organizations including Amazon, Google, Mayo Clinic, PayPal, DoorDash, and more. He holds a Doctorate in Organizational Leadership, an MBA, an MPH, and an ICF PCC credential.

Ben is the author of Becoming Fearless and the creator of Becoming, a self-leadership app built on the same philosophy. He hosts the Live Fearlessly and The Executive podcasts and is a regular speaker on leadership, self-trust, and navigating career transitions.

Born and raised in Chicago, Illinois, Ben now resides in Austin, Texas, with his wife, Tiffany, Squirt, a "rebel in a shell" turtle, Elwood, a scruffy rescue pup, and Sima, the kitty queen of their kingdom.

He also loves hearing from his readers, feel free to send an email to benjaminritter@lfyconsulting.com and learn more at Liveforyourselfconsulting.com.

Additionally, please tell other readers why you liked this book by reviewing it on Amazon or Goodreads.

Your review could inspire others to become fearless. If you do write a review, please send Ben an email so he can thank you personally.

www.ingramcontent.com/pod-product-compliance
Lightning Source LLC
Chambersburg PA
CBHW051445130726
47987CB00005B/2194